Archive Avenue

Aneek Chatterjee

Introduction

"Archive Avenue" consists of seventy one poems between its covers, all written in free verse. A few prose poems have been sheltered in its pages. Many of these poems were published earlier in leading literary magazines and poetry anthologies across the globe. Poems in this collection were mostly composed in 2020 and 2021. "Archive Avenue" is the fourth poetry collection authored by me.

This anthology has two sections, themed 'Mindscape' and 'Pandemic'. I believe that many of my compositions, if not all, belong to the mindscape of the author. These are, in many instances, inward looking; although they traverse to different terrains in the outer world. But they come back and get a perfect abode in the inner space. Therefore the first section themed 'Mindscape' has poems hovering around the author's psyche, his conscious and subconscious, his feelings and observations about the known milieu and the unknown.

Poets and poems are products of their times. Can an author, writing now, evade the ubiquitous impact of Covid 19, the pandemic that has made our lives vastly different in recent times? The scourge of the pandemic, which has been tormenting us since the late 2019, still exists. A number of poems included in this collection, therefore, refer to the pandemic, in the second section of the book.

Readers and critics are the best judges of an author. Three of my earlier poetry collections, titled "Seaside Myopia" (Cyberwit, 2018); "Unborn Poems and Yellow Prison" (Cyberwit, 2019) and "Of Ashes and Persiflage" (Hawakal, 2020) received encouraging response from readers and rave reviews from literary critics. Such responses and reviews provided sustainable fodders for this anthology.

Dr. Karunesh Kumar Agrawal of Cyberwit.net deserves huge thanks for bringing out another poetry collection of mine with utmost care and sincerity. I am extremely satisfied with the quality production of this volume, like the previous ones. As always, my wife Sarbani and daughter Prerna provided necessary oxygen, for this work also. Without their cooperation, this anthology would not have materialized. Finally, if the readers accept "Archive Avenue", I will consider my efforts worthy.

Aneek Chatterjee

19 August, 2022

Acknowledgements

I express my sincere gratitude to the editors of different literary magazines and anthologies for publishing many poems included in this anthology. Poet Fred of *Ann Arbor Review*, Vera Ignatowitsch of *Better Than Starbucks*, Steve Cawte of *Imspired Magazine*, William S. Peters, Sr. of Innerchild Press, Sand Pilarski of *Piker Press*, Mark A. Murphy of *Poetica Review*, Amit Permessur of *The Pangolin Review,* Quaz Roodt of *Poetry Potion*, Aminur Rahman of *Dhaka Review*, Sunil Sharma and Gopal Lahiri of *Voices Within* (of *"Setu"*) Rajesh Subramanian of *Modern Literature*, Glory Sasikala of *GloMag*, Kiriti Sengupta of *Hibiscus*, Pranab Ghosh of *Existential Problems*, Sreetanwi Chakraborty of *Tech Touch Talk* and *Kafe House* and the Editor of *Trouvaille Review*

Contents

Section 2 67

Section 1

MINDSCAPE

Nascent Bylanes

Hanging in front
Red yellow blue orange green
in the paper board.
Take a gun in hand
& shoot as per desire
Shoot my id, my pretence, lust,
ladder, arrogance

Be a sharp shooter
& shoot, as per desire
all pumped balloons
hanging from the
ephemeral board

But do not shoot
nascent lanes & bylanes
beside the bush
Tomorrow
red yellow blue orange
paths may sprout from
nowhere

Carcass

The carcass of the turtle
touched my feet on the shore
in a dark cloudy morning

A group of innocent plastics
blocked my drain, the way we
raised demands on the road

Trees whispered to me their souls when
I slowly walked to the court of
emperor Chandragupta. They're dumb now.

& heavy air told me in a
twenty first century afternoon:
contact, if you wish to poison wish

I rushed back, and murmured
to the carcass, pardon my desire,
forgive our arrogance

The sea laughed loud
& drew me towards the front;
I walked, walked, till I was lost

My carcass looked amused on the shore

Dance Floor

I organize a dance party
inside, the floor is lighted,
people come & go
Many dance with me,
ceaseless
But some only watch
ruins, only lament famine
outside

Let the world die silently
Those who deserve death, must
die, those who can't dance will
develop unfit toes & legs
Those who shy away from light
must remain in darkness

I don't want to come out
of my bones, flesh & skin.
Inside dazzles in light, dance,
laughter.
It's full of flowing crops
giggling in the sun, with power
to supress any famine
outside

Space

In between two lines
I'm the lonely sike
looking at the sky,
looking at my bones & flesh.
Did I go wrong, when
those lines suddenly caught
fire with schism?

I'm flowing through marshy
lands, mud in body
Give me space between banks

Dry due to excessive
heat
In between two lines,
invoke some rains

Archive Avenue

Sometimes I pause on
archive avenue & dig a
laced football that required
pumping in bladder, careful stitch
& ten obliterated kids.
A neighbor's banters
& howling hummed in
mind; ghosts on
green lakes, guarded by
nonsense trees, prowled
freely.

Sometimes I pause on a
page where a lunatic
is busy
reversing the calendar

Passion

Bat swirled around the
attic, and the high walls
of the red prison.
Batman was climbing
the hills.
Passions always differ.
Tough wall meets the blue sky
& they only changed positions

Now the small attic is comfortable
for the resting bat

Rituals

My heart beats fast
half a kilometer before the train station
Every day at the junction, a terrible traffic jam
mocks the morning sun
& the lady with scarlet red lips
throws me a kiss from the lamppost
I want to hang myself in.

My day started at 8 a.m.
for the 9.08 EMU
Throughout the road, I'd devoured
TMT pipes, witty butters, solid vests,
dream apartments & lucrative bras
& met the scarlet- lip woman.

It's already 8.50, and the last eighteen minutes
make me a great chartered accountant,
I see at the junction with a blue shirt
& thin moustache.
If I get the EMU, my birth has some meaning;
If not, I'll go back to the lamppost,
kiss the woman
& hang myself …

To be born again at 8 a.m.
tomorrow

Giggles

Mother laughs in the corner of
my now open heart
I stretch my eyes in tandem
with the black wire,
but all vanish into the oblivion
A few fairies come back along the
dark route
& whisper fairy tales
& mother helps them with
more exciting fables
I try to open my eyes
to rescue her sullied recipe
but they are lost,
in oblivion

& in a white bed, I hear
fairy giggles

Allusion

Believed i was there, on the podium
But you said it wasn't me

The train had left station in the
afternoon. The concert began
in the woods, colorful leaves
adorned the autumn,
red, yellow
& some mauve flowers.
The podium was dazzling

At one lonely row, last,
nobody was around,
he came to taste the concert.
The train crossed a river
by the bank of which evening
concerts were held, intimate
singers & intimate listeners

The train essayed over the bridge
& the piano started;
he longed to hear from the last row
but the arrogant guitar rushed
to the podium

Give me a break, give me a
stoppage, this train runs too
fast, like the forgotten yellow
car

The woods are full of music
I wish to hear before dusk

When evening descended,
i was on the podium
But you said it wasn't
me

Yellow Bush

This morning red flowers
bloomed in dark inviting clouds

Decided all of a sudden to fly
& invade the darkness

& get drenched in all accumulated
water particles we call rains,

when dropped on earth. & I started
flying past the yellow bush that

dripped painting on the roadside.
& treacherous rains started showering.

Yellow bush smiled at my plight
& threw colored waves to a dark

chamber I nurtured inside for so many
years. Now I'm getting drenched

inside the yellow bush, like a teenager
who fell in love for the first time in life

The Smile

You don't look like the photograph
the pale wall hangs so preciously.
Spiders had eaten up the lips
bit by bit in three decades
you were at war, with yourself, your body,
you thought decorated with
scents of jasmine and boned with steel.
The bamboo leaf nose was lost
in the last storm, from a blow that
was natural, yet unnatural
from a fist you'd faith in.
And clouds from the storm nestled
on the shelter below your eyes
Three decades have seen a lot of
changes; we transformed
from pranksters to office hoppers
We landed and felt landed in our
fantasies, bodies we admired
and hated; eyes we loved to be lost in.
We never knew insects kiss and care
our precious bodies in the wall
after three decades of war; we
finally lost to spiders and lizards,
when the smile looked like
weeping in front

This Road

Where does this road go?
It goes through my mind to
the mystery jungle, where I
bloom like a yellow flower
& feel soft butterflies.
It goes up the hill where I
kiss the clouds & bathe inside
rains; where I am the yet-to-be
named orchid. It goes to the blue
sea to make me a marine life
in the world of colorful fishes.
I play with them in the warm zone.
This road also goes to a crematorium
in the heart of the city, where in a wintry
evening I bid adieu my brother
& felt like ashes in the burning pyre.
This road goes through narrow by-lanes
where struggle for existence gets
cinematic, and some real heroes are born
everyday.
This road makes my sojourn
endless, timeless too

Skeleton

I paint the skeleton with all
possible colors,
marrow and flesh
Through its eyes green grass
are visible, and the paper,
left in the rear seat of the car

Time is just a vacuum.
You can refill it in your mind,
recreate cranky shoes
and the gentle sound
of the car door ;
the road and the lawn,
along the side of which
the car sped …

Never to be recreated again.

Colors

Colors have many tales…

Long back a friend said
he loved yellow teeth
Sometimes truth came out
of yellow teeth, he felt
white only smiled, emotions
& truth remained within

After polls, red turned green.
Of those who remained red,
few proud radicals practiced
incredible somersault
in green rooms.
They will vault & vault to
other dynamic colors,
after every change

Hence the friend said,
see dark in every color.
Ruthless cynic.

Fascinating colors
confused me, always.

Home

At the beginning believed
home. A scrutiny beneath
revealed cracking,
molten wood
The still eyes of the feral
returned, throwing live
queries.
& all my prates
ably discovered by you
from inside the glass rack.
Summer had long eloped
but the floor was still
burning.

On the road now
neighboring white snow,
fully sated

Ghost Hunter

I walk in the main street,
in broad day light.
I'm the ghost hunter,
with a big sack on my back,
& some amount of
money in my purse
I meet many ghosts in society
tall, short, thin, fat, well dressed,
well groomed,
undressed skeletons & more …
They greet me, talk to me
& accept money I offer
to be in my sack.

But I haven't got a single ghost
in main street, lanes & bylanes

Now my skeleton laughs at me,
as I jump into my empty sack

Soliloquies

Cacophony in the air,
& life was too vibrant
outside our small, crowded stall,
where we assembled
to read poems.
A lady was shouting in
an open stage, someone
was selling his product;
others were busy announcing
programs, loud.
But we were determined to
continue
We read, we read …
& continued reading;
but could not hear any poet,
anything
Our microphone felt nervous at
the beginning, and then went silent.
We read soliloquies in a crowd

and after each reading,
we clapped our existence.

Invisible Eyes

Two invisible eyes, dark red
or black or yellow, or whatever
you imagine,
scanning our existence, our daily
chores.

Long ago when humanity
was learning,
two indigestible words
appeared:
Demos, Kratos …
These were supposed to
help your voice, your wish
to let the world know
your agony,
despair, marginalization

We're learned now
Time has changed
& also, art of living …

Visit art galleries, shopping malls
Eat drink & be merry
Shout,
but don't barf the indigestible

Two eyes multiplied into
thousands now,
& scanning our
sick brains

Dead Men

When I see dead men
crossing potholes with smile ...
I see smiles clouded in mystery.

When I see mystery in every act
& every action drowned
in broken roads,
potholes,
I accompany dead men
in their journey to survival

Hideout

Don't want to know
where I am
Absconding from masks
and musketeers,
in a hideout
somewhere.
Absconding from murky
roads to chair
From butter and knives
From glitter and smiles,
play and players

It has markets nearby
where people come and go
A theater, several pubs
and restaurants, schools
and hospitals

Don't want to know about
my hideout
Instead take a plunge
Inside
and search the dark
chamber

Coffee Cup, Red Cherries

A big meteorite is circling
& mocking everyday sojourn
Treacherous drops of the ocean
jump to my coffee cup
My toes, rhythms with girlfriend
finally dance to a splendid vacuity.
& I respond to calls from red cherries
but a Coelurosauria threatening me
from nowhere
Pubs are full of creatures I haven't
seen in my plate before, eating
every bit of my food
The fork has only joined the ugly
passage of the meteorite

Red cherries still calling...
But my coffee cup has
surrendered to the
Coelurosauria

When I Woke Up

I saw my house from the hills
It was surrounded by mist,
like my dream

And I descended through the forests,
through hazy mist
to enter a known world

But the brown door vanished
in the mist full of vengeance
when I woke up in dreams

Evening

Death will come inevitable
like rains in a black evening
Music will go on, our likes &
dislikes, our treachery &
magnanimity, our revelry &
obscenity,
mask & nudity

The team of immortals has been
announced, & glad that I'm
deservedly out. Now it's time
to write my obituary, happily
in a whiskey evening

Framed

I have a limited sky
inside and out of the framed
window
Through it I watch twilight,
dust and storm,
a naked tree full of naughty
crows
Through it I watch people
and the road
The road, someone said
flows into a river
I haven't seen

I thought of a great storm
that would throw my window
to the river
But that did not happen
I imagined green leaves
on the tree
They never appeared
I wanted the naughty crow
to be less noisy
for at least a day;
and people on the road
to wave at each other,

I wanted to see the
whole sky painted pink or
gold or crimson with my desire

But could
not make my window
come out
of the fixed frame,
a single day

A Grasshopper Jumps

I present my gloom in a
packet of wondering flowers.
Sighs of agony melt
in the skies, above green
forest.
A grasshopper jumps into
the innermost space of my
cardiac chamber and says,
throw your last breaths
to a frolicking children's
park, in the dazzle of
cosmic rays …

in a sudden dusk

Searching Moments

Truths we dislike and
avoid; bitter, sweeter,
funny
But truths come back
to us, obstinate, more at
midnight, but often at
other times
They keep prying through
us, naked
We try to escape
with costly,
ordinary covers,
in vain …
They pierce through
pretensions, perfume
and wit, ballooned logic

The truth is nobody
wants to die,
But everybody
dies regularly, in
solitary, searching moments

Summit

The man coming down the hills
informed that he could not stay
at the top long enough because
sharp - edged stones that formed a throne-like
landscape there pricked, and the summit
lacked adequate oxygen for survival.

Secrets

Secrets are a bundle
of philosophy we taste
sometimes in life

The open book
scripting our journey
on road smiles in shadow

The Picture

Amid swinging drizzle, I saw a child on the footpath, with a paper in his hand. It showed a colorful picture which drew me close. The head of a mule was trapped in between gaps of a chair. The ass was trying hard to pull out its head free, but it couldn't. The child was intensely looking at the image and laughing profusely, all by himself. The chair looked costly, high quality, with exquisite designs. The donkey, nobody knew why, was attracted to the chair and put its head in between the splendid curves and got stuck. Or it could be the other way. The chair came closer to the ass. The child found the whole episode quite funny and pointed towards the pic when I approached.

Honestly, as an adult I didn't find out what was so funny in the picture.

Friday Locusts

Sat numb in the coffee house in a friday evening, locusts whirling ... Your red attire flew outside the window to the unknown sky. The sandwich appeared out of a traffic junction I got stuck in several times. Insects informed it was actually a geometry lesson I hated in school. Wanted to jump in the black hole inside the cup, but your stretched hand by the side was a solid branch I was not in a trance breaking. Instead, my brain sent a few locusts to sip quickly the unsavory taste of the black hole. But it remained. The triangular suddenly transformed into liquid. Locusts informed it happens when dusty layers of the brain become dysfunctional or when water is poured into it & someone sits numb in the enchanting friday evening dreaming red. Only the window opened to black by-lanes.

Intersections

First point of intersection was a desert; smoky hot sand green nails couldn't withstand. I wanted to pour water. But the crude & hot sand thought I wanted to pour water. Sand dunes looked aghast as the vacuum slowly returned, dejected. Rocky was a better term for the second. I watched a stone where no moss had ever appeared & the scarlet red attire was truly fumbling. Started feeling cherries inside green leaves. Wanted to pluck in haste and the giggle stopped; dry bones appeared instead. Brown they all were. The lonely stone laughed loud only this time. Since then, journeying incessantly on endless roads, without any sight of intersections

Mahogany Dark

The sturdy, decorated chair
melted like chocolate in my
mouth.
I was in awe, when I sighted
the gorgeous chair and the
dignified presence
of the ephemeral figure.
My mouth opened up
automatically;
& I felt the chair melting …,
melting fast in saliva

The mahogany dark chocolate
tasted like any ordinary one
I had outside school, in
times of yore.
But now I chewed it cautiously,
lest I fell sick.
& devoured it instant.

Only the chair observed
from a distance

Alien

In one corner of the world
I spread my wings, happy like a butterfly.
The president smiles from the currency
notes all adore back home
My white collar has turned yellow
for targets.
Butterflies, orange and white,
also spread their wings in the thick,
thorny bush where tiny flowers
offered irresistible nectar to children,
who knew the flowers like close relatives,
uncle and aunts, providing mangoes,
mired in milk and bread in hot
summer evenings

Uncle Sam watches me invisible when
I bite my bread with cucumber and sausage
I bought with smiling currency notes
The thorny bush is also smiling from
within a white collar migrant
in an alien, dreamland.

Mirror

Through my glass window
I look at the uprooted tree,
a victim of the last storm
now lying stoic on the road,
lazily watching bicycles, motorbikes
& pedestrians passing by.
This tree was home to several birds,
electric & cable wires; political posters.
Now uprooted & lying peacefully

I withdrew from the window
& came inside
Suddenly in the mirror saw
a banyan tree in front of a
village house & children playing
beneath

I withdrew again &
stopped looking
at the mirror, because
it was looking through me

Pains

Pains have many exits,
but only a single depository,
hidden inside bones.
In that invisible pot, the old lady
unloads lonely winter evenings
in candle light.
Here the barren fields whisper
melancholy after every harvest
& wrinkles around doused eyes
practice laughter surreptitiously.

Pains have many languages,
but only one page
where we scribble colored
graphs of monitors from
white, cold beds.

Pains have many becks,
but only one small pond,
where drops are stored
in winter & fall, spring
& summer

Colored Graphs

Colored graphs of the monitor
dancing in front of
white, cold bed.
19th century ceiling fans
have been replaced
recently
But the long iron rods supporting
new, sleek fans
in the ancient room
bring back lost history, long
enough like hanging rods.
I silently appreciate all dancing
graphs in front; symbols of survival,
symbols of light for the man
in a cold, white bed

Destination

This metro runs fast
under the city, noiseless.
People are engrossed in their
phones, certain about their
destinations.

I was also certain about my
destination
But I never knew rains
don't splash on you
under the city, relations don't
touch in the heart of the city,
laughters are lost in the ephemeral
bubbles from the beer mug

Now I feel uncertain about
my destination.

Before 'Nirvana'

When I close my eyes for a 'nirvana', —
kind of eternal peace I love to seek,
insects whirl in my mind
& brain, — insects of different
forms & shape & actions.

My id wears a swim suit & jumps into
the pool of desire. The lady comes out of the
pond of a coffee cup I used to hold in front
of the red attire in friday evenings,
in the crowded coffee house, before it
melted into the blue.
Weeds surrounding me looked like
innocent leaves and flowers
I dreamed when I visited the garden of
Eden. & in that garden, in a lovely lake
you floated in the coffee cup,
without clothes

Blue is my color of desire, blue is
the color of my clouds of thought.
& my id, my untold passion, my ego float
like big insects in swimsuit.

Before any 'Nirvana', take me, therefore,
through a phase known as brain death.

Arrivals

Arrivals are always hazy,
morning mist.
Patience takes a beating
like the hapless child on pavement,
waiting for boiled rice.
Arrivals are seldom, like
the flower that blooms once in
every fourteen years.
But expectations have some
irresistible aroma, you are drawn to
like a possessed soul.
The aroma keeps you travel
in the barren, harvested field
in a melancholic, winter evening.

Outsider

Fresh sapling in between stones,
outsider, looking up to
feel the sun.
The sun is an
outsider too, here in this
planet.
I don't have that charisma,
I don't have that energy,
& the power to enlighten every
mind.
Waiting like an outsider,
if you bend down a bit
if you come & sit on the stone
& if I receive a splash of that
irresistible odour.
Waiting in anxiety, pain,
with newly composed love
tunes,
if you recognize the outsider
in between stones
& tunes

The Blue Moon

The blue moon smiled and posed for
different angles, different lenses,
locations and moods.

A line escaped from my friend's poem
captioned: 'from my dark balcony
in a bright autumn evening'.

A relative in a faraway land
wondered why it was blue!
But he hailed the spectacular dazzle.

A mariner sent me golden
liquid, supposed to be blue,
but golden aplenty.

At midnight, i observed lonely close
And found it blue, absolutely
blue, in lens blurred by indignity, shame

Locked Existence

You think of the future & the shadow
becomes lengthier enough to devour
the exciting & magnificent today.

Tiny pebbles are structured by the sea
for the great edifice; a boisterous
wave comes dancing to play with it.

Pebbles consume time, from dawn
to afternoon, but the evening descends
suddenly, like the wave; and silhouette

we become from our beaming selves
in sunlight, in joy & ecstasy,
in sands, brown & white.

You paint the door of the locker
silvery bright, for a dazzle in dark, but light
escapes unnoticed for locked existence.

You

In a faraway land
I search for words,
in boulevards, by-lanes
when you evolve

In my native village
green paddy fields swing
in air, sunshine
when you evolve

In my birth I first
felt you, in school my verse
carried you to earth
in a cloudy morning, in march

Syllabus in college was
you; syllables you,
And in a busy office, the
wooden desk, unknown file, you

In near and far
In paddy fields, and
boulevards, in birth and daily
death, only you evolve

Lost Book, Purple Sweater

Now I close the door
Now I close all windows
Put out all lights in the pathway.
Now I darken the moon
Now I darken the brain
to see those who walked
the green grass in misty mornings;
who sang winning songs
beside the piano; who lighted the
stove in the kitchen in winter
nights.
Now I see the coffee cup
& the lost book; the purple sweater
with long hands, long enough to
reach a broad shoulder.
Now I see my sister plucking
yellow flowers, now I see friends
in the football ground

Now I close all doors, all windows
to be eligible to see everything
in front of my dead eyes

Our Tales

At the end of the day
I see a flattening curve.
All ups and downs have
plummeted to dust.
All colored, dreamy mounds
are whispering to yellow grass
their final, infructuous tales.
& those who sighed minus tags,
have now prepared beds on dust
& grass, by the side of
tips of pyramids.
All curves are now flattened
Only the setting sun has a glorious,
cryptic smile

Victory

Those who want to win
let them be winners …
Some victories stand on
deceit & tears & shame
Some joys melt in hard
stones in gloomy afternoons
A mad rush to the podium
fails to listen
to the whispers of dust
& grass; the agony of dashing
air accompanying you

If you still want to run,
you'll reach & adorn the podium
only to discover that your run
is incomplete
& the white starting line,
supposedly straight,
looks curved from here, with you
at the tip
of an embarrassed curve

Lost Species

Visited the graveyard
in a winter evening
& buried many of my poems
there.
They never homed my
body cells, my semi dark mind,
pale white nails,
closed eyes.

Fossil poems were like
lost dinosaurs, this graveyard
sheltered for million years …
They never crushed me, they never
won me; they
were never pieces of magnets.

Let them be lost species
in this lost graveyard,
I visit now & then.

Melting Afternoon

Reading your book now,
which I first opened
thousand years ago with
a bit of trepidation.
But I discover soft afternoons
mellowed in caramel ice creams.
Some yellow leaves, some black stones,
some known tunes & many smiles.
I remember the pebbles on the boulevard
& the motor bike that sped past
the Mars in a summer morning.
Celestial bodies, you perhaps know,
are my favorites, always.
I see green grass and orange flowers
on them & all favorite colors here,
on earth.

This book has its blood with the soil
of earth, the smell of rustic iron,
the air of innocent arrogance.

Turning over another page
& a black hole sucking me inside
mellowed ice cream,
in this melting afternoon.

Locusts

I search words…
Words laugh from my back,
from my sides, left and right.
They laugh from the rack; hang from
ceiling, chairs and the
silent mirror.

I search words;
But find an incessant flow
of locusts to a dusty brain,
I've watched die silently.
Long ago.

Horizon

In the horizon I see black birds
perched on dry branches of a tree
and
red clouds threatening
life below. It's always possible to
spread fear when you're above,
partnering black birds, cruel and naked
branches.

I am waiting far below, far from the sky.
But
I know sky is a big vacuum, sky is too vast
to absorb threats, fear, hatred
and hope; and a long distance surveyor.

Here I am, waiting far below, looking at the horizon
to spot a white bird, green leaves, red flowers.
Here I am, stirring the horizon to dissolve fear,
hatred and threats in the ultimate pot;
for some yet-to- smile discovery.

The Wood

The wood or the stone
you found had small ripples inside, or
great surging waves to clear any dirty shore; or
gentle air that transmitted oxygen to souls.
Winters were claustrophobic in the town;
in the small alleys, with 17th century hanging bulbs.
And when you melted in the face opposite; your painted lips
drew undeciphered scripts on the newly discovered stone.

Surging waves only rolled back
behind the wood, faceless.

Million Years

Took brisk & big steps
on the sea beach
& covered many, many miles.
Every grain of sand was accompanying.
& I witnessed a meteor hit me, hit earth
& the sea was surging
Hoards of dinosaurs jumped on the beach
& smells of fish, moss, salty water
gradually overpowered me.
Fifty million years smiled.

When I tasted salty water,
I found my door open.

Empty Triangle

Two plus two makes four
in simple arithmetic.
But here is a unique geometry, of a triangle
& a square which lives within the triangle …
Four souls in four distant, but joined
points of the empty square.

Two plus two always makes four.
But it may also lead to four hundred;
four thousand; four million; — our smiles, our joy,
our afternoons, rains & spring, venom & nectar.
An empty square lives within an empty triangle …
You, me, he. Rains, spring & winter; —
joined, but alienated.

A Long Road

The name I knew quickly disappeared
The game I played was forgotten
The fame they coveted, jeered.

A long road was sleeping silently when
we met, — seemingly unaware of footsteps;
of raindrops and blazing rays, proud cavalcades.

I asked the name; wanted the game;
it didn't respond. When I was about to
return after a long sojourn, it whispered:

give me raindrops; give me the blazing sun;
give me colors by the side. Everything else,
footsteps and cavalcades, I sleep away, for pain.

Section 2

PANDEMIC

Full Stops

We're now inside,
looking into our bones & flesh

to peel off the silver
& protein of audacious id

Nights move into days
& days into nights

We don't laugh anymore,
Or if we do, it's lost

in black masks or yellow,
or white, we're now showing !

Never tried to feel green pains,
agony of the road, of birds, puzzled sky

Megalomania never knew how we
leapfrogged dues, wise existence

Now all days & all chilled nights
are rewardingly ponderous, full stops

Corona

Show your stockpile
of weapons of mass destruction
to corona,
it will laugh silently
Show your sophisticated war planes
and submarines, it will
mock
Show your 50, 60, 100 floor
skyscrapers, it will fly
there

& from the top,
advice you,
humans,
think fresh, think anew
There was
something wrong with your
ideas

Quarantine Muses

Rains have come after all,
in times of trouble

Wet green leaves invited
me for a swing in rains

Despite rains, I got burnt in a
vibrant forest of unsuspecting flowers

Pink yellow red & blue colored
a reluctant tabula rasa this holi

& in a March morning, I whispered
to Aparajita leaves in the balcony

Tell the world I'm still doing fine
Although in quarantine

Puja & Pandemic

Durga Ma looked from her
upper pedestal at me &
the surroundings.
Lights were glittering everywhere;
& the majestic chandelier throwing its
aura & kindness. The red & golden pandal,
with intricate art work depicting a part of
a glorious Indian tradition, was also
shining above & under the magnificent
chandelier.
Ma, along with her lovable children,
smiling.
Suddenly I felt a vacuum inside,
like the deserted pandal, barricaded under
legal directives.

Puja started, the priest, in white dhoti,
was chanting holy mantra in all seriousness
I stood there empty
I observed blind
& saw the whole pandal
under a big black mask

The Flame

Pink petals of Cherry were waving at us
through silver drizzles in a march morning.
They call it Sakura
Some fallen, wet petals of Sakura were
guiding us along the green grass

We were on a journey to the Flame,
The ever igniting flame of
Hiroshima

& we saw the bricks, the wall
& the burning flame; — burning, yet benign,
signalling the triumph of humanity

Hydrozen bombs were not enough
to drowse the flame.

Have you seen it burning, Corona ?

Pestilence

Silence had a rhythm
earlier
But when it is everywhere,
the big avenue weeps
& red ants whisper inside.
The naked tree only houses
black crows, drowsy
Known faces look cinematic
under a visible mask
This silence is devoid of
syllables,
only pestilence knows

Midday Sun

Come, let us draw a sun, like we used to
in our childhood. A circle & several short lines around.
Two eyes on the up inside the circle
Remember, we used to color the circle
red or yellow, depending on our mood.
Now we know that red is for dawn, dusk
& yellow is midday sun, burning on our shoulders

Let us invoke the powerful midday sun again
to drive away all gloom, all despair,
all uncertainty surrounding us this time.

Did you say midday sun wasn't enough
for corona? I'll tell you it was only a simulacrum
of strength our painting, music & poetry have
to obliterate all gloom from the earth

Change

Life will not be the same again
after corona, they said

& I came back to my escape,
& poured melancholy in white pillow

A Koel whistled in childhood
& friends suddenly became explorers

Soothing breeze came through
the rectangle, with nagging fragrance of *Jui*

& my escape whispered: the world
will not be the same again; it'll better

Summer Evening

Sea laughs hundred kilometers
from mind.
Flowers are far, far away.
The venus and the half baked moon
seemed nearer on this
pestilence awed evening.

Sea breeze suddenly swept
me away; yellow flowers
bloomed in all trees
kissing my terrace.
And the venus smiled:
'I took away fear, agony;
you only spread your wings
in the breeze'.

I started to fly in
a summer evening.

Hillock

There was no oxygen cylinder
I did not complaint
There was no medicine
I did not protest
There was no bed in hospitals
I was indifferent
There was no sympathy in the air
I took it as natural.

In a summer evening,
I looked through the window
and found a smiling moon …

Over a hillock
of piling dead bodies.

They were looking through
me
and complaining, in silence.

N 95

Masks you preferred,
in market, on road, inside offices,
schools & universities
You had so many things to say,
you'd so many issues to protest
You wanted to jeer, cry, laugh loud
but masks prevented you
Masks reminded you: behave, somebody's
watching with stick & carrot

Corona unmasked you, your suppressed lump,
your soliloquies, your social face.
Dear humans, you're finally caught
red handed
under N 95

Festival

Blood that splashed into my mind,
reached tin - doors, mud-walls;
roofs of thatched houses.

Fire that engulfed rival party offices,
set ablaze mass funerals of
covid kissed bodies, here and there.

Election to the legislature got over
recently. Seats to the avowed edifice
had been booked.

Pandemic reached every door,
tinned and wooden,
decorated and ordinary.

Everybody surrendered to unprecedented
awe. Only the fire was celebrating a festival
of death; only blood reached mind, roofs

in silence. And I suddenly discovered
all seats in the legislature
resembled pale, dried blood.

Another Year

Yellow flowers are back,
back in abundance, shining,
exactly after a year.

At this time last year, the pandemic
came to our doors & we were
horrified, frustrated & confined.

The yellow flowers bloomed &
smiled at me from a neighboring
tree, sheltering buoyant birds.

They chirped, flew, came back
to nests, made little pranks with
yellow flowers, siblings.

They waved at me, they sang to me.
My boredom, confinement flew to the tree
& yellow flowers carefully nested them.

Welcome back, sunshine.
Welcome back vibrancy & life.
Another year has passed & we're smiling again.

Hope

When mud covered
bones & flesh in days of yore,
sudden rains splashed joy, hope

The lonely beck meandering through
marshy lands without ease
always cheered me

When the drowsy road felt guilty
for pestilence, yellow bushes dripped
painting & whispered love

The milkyway told in an orange evening
hope is not just a four letter word,
it's found everywhere in the galaxy

Summer

When first cries from
Wuhan crossed the Great Wall,
Don't know why
I was reminded of Gustav Klimt
& his 'Death and Life',
where death on the left patiently
watching the celebration of life
on the right.
Celebration, in all possible colors …
Mothers holding aloft
new born babies,
men and women embracing
the taste of life.

Death with an ugly skull
watching
& waiting patiently for his
turn, which he knew
would surely come

When a lady was put on ventilator
in Bergamo, signals from
the white Alps
reverberated around the world
& life plunged to
assist life

When the ugly skull laughed
& took away some,

more & more came out of the
clutches of death

& now after a few months, when
I know that smiles outnumbered
coffins, I was reminded of a laborious work
of Pieter Brueghel, the Younger:
Spring, —
which painted a community
joining hands to prepare the soil,
plant seeds & readying the livestock again
in a lively village

Waiting for that warm
summer to arrive once more.

Vacuum

Intricacies have turned
virtual in the new normal
Sure you won't call me a cad
now if I lovingly throw
you in the air
inside my cell phone
& send the best picture of
a peart somebody,
essay a poem effortless
into your brain.

But show me please,
how can I paint
a ubiquitous vacuum
in the virtual space,
in a new normal ?

Stone Evening

I'm alone on the road,
walking through the pandemic

& drowsy yellow flowers, hesitant
for a great bloom at this time.

Evening wishes to descend with
a red face, on shy wet asphalt

A lazy shower dripped
prohibition in days of yore

Where are you heading ? A vulture
abandoned the rat, disgruntled

The road provided no answer,
neither could i in a stone evening